HALFTIME WITH DON

Ken Weitzman

I0139722

BROADWAY PLAY PUBLISHING INC
New York
www.broadwayplaypublishing.com
info@broadwayplaypublishing.com

HALFTIME WITH DON
© Copyright 2021 Ken Weitzman

Cover image from the B Street Theatre production by Barry Crider, Lunia Blue

First edition: March 2021
I S B N: 978-0-88145-896-1

Book design: Marie Donovan
Page make-up: Adobe InDesign
Typeface: Palatino

HALFTIME WITH DON was developed during a residency at the Eugene O'Neill Theater Center's National Playwrights Conference (Preston Whiteway, Executive Director; Wendy C Goldberg, Artistic Director) in 2015.

HALFTIME WITH DON was first produced as a National New Play Network Rolling World Premiere by New Jersey Repertory Company (New Jersey), the Phoenix Theatre (Indiana), and B Street Theatre (California)

The cast and creative contributors for the New Jersey Repertory Company (SuzAnne Barabas, Artistic Director; Gabor Barabas, Executive Producer) production, running from 22 June-30 July 2017 were:

DON ....Malachy Cleary
STEPHANIE.. Lori Vega
ED...Dan McVey
SARAH...Susan Maris

Director .... Kent Nicholson
Set design .... Jessica Parks
Lighting design .... Jill Nagle
Costume design .... Patricia E Doherty
Fight Director .... Brad Lemons
Sound design........................... Merek Royce Press
Production Stage Manager ....Kristin Pfeifer
Assistant Stage Manager..............................Adam von Pier
Assistant Director............................ Lindy Regan

The cast and creative contributors for the Phoenix Theatre (Bryan Fonseca, Artistic Director) production, running from 12 January-4 February 2018, were:

DON .... Bill Simmons
STEPHANIE .... Lauren Briggeman
SARAH .... Chelsea Anderson
ED .... Michael Hosp

Director .... Bryan Fonseca
Set design .... Daniel Udhe
Lighting design .... Laura Glover
Costume design .... Brittany Kugler
Sound design .... Ben Dobler
Production Stage Manager .... Danielle Buckel
Assistant Director .... Corbin Fritz

The cast and creative contributors for the B Street Theatre (Buck Busfield, Producing Artistic Director, Jerry Montoya Executive Producer) production, running from, 15-30 December 2018, were:

DON ....Rich Hebert
STEPHANIE.......................................Danielle Mone Truitt
ED...Dave Pierini
SARAH...Tate Hanyok

Director .... Buck Busfield
Set design ....Samantha Reno
Lighting design ....Dylan Ballestero
Costume design ....Shelley Riley
Stage Manager .... Veronica Sprague
Production Assistant .... Kelsey Hammontree

Special thanks to Nan Barnett, Jordana Fraider and whole crew at N N P N, and to the organizations, in addition to the O'Neill, where the play was developed: Premiere Stages, the Playwrights Center, Theatre Lab at F A U, City Theatre Company, and the Lark.

And a special thank you to two important advocates, for this play and for my work all along: Wendy Goldberg and Christian Parker.

And, as always, Amy. Who's been here for it all.

CHARACTERS

DON DEVERS, *ex-N F L player. Mid-50s. Big personality. Big, boisterous laugh, charming. Which can turn instantly to volcanic anger. Despite his condition/circumstances, he never gives in to pain or even a shred of self-pity. He doesn't have to be huge, or match today's NF L standards. He was a defensive back or linebacker decades ago. Different time, different bodies. There's much wiggle room here.*

STEPHANIE DEVERS, *early to mid-30s.* DON's *daughter. Pregnant, almost due. Tough, crass, unapologetic, but with deep and desperate feeling for her father coursing beneath it.*

ED RYAN, 40. *Trying, trying so hard, never stops trying. Battling to still believe in possibility. Awed by* DON. *Married to* SARAH.

SARAH RYAN, *mid-30s. Pregnant, mid-second trimester. Married to* ED. *Trying so hard to be supportive, to encourage and urge* ED *along, and to cover her panic.*

A note on casting: Any ethnicity, race, etc. For DON, *do look at the makeup of the N F L. He is most likely either African-American or White.*

SETTING

The world: DON's *condo and* STEPHANIE's *condo respectively. Maybe these spaces are detailed and fully realized, maybe each is comprised of a single set piece, creating islands of isolation. Whatever is chosen, it's very important the play moves from one scene to the other fluidly, quickly, without breaks, blackouts, or waiting for scene changes.*

Punctuation: A double-dash at the end of a sentence indicates it's cut-off by the next line. Ellipses is the character stopping or trailing off from not knowing what to say next or how to articulate it or just hesitating to give voice to the thought. It shouldn't have dialogue added to it.

ACT ONE

Scene 1

(A beat-up recliner. Tipped all the way back. All we see are the soles of two feet covered by well-worn tube socks. We sit with this image for a beat, then…a doorbell.)

(We see the feet on the recliner stir.)

(Lights up on ED—*geeked out, excited, and awkward anticipation—stands outside the door [though perhaps there's no literal door].)*

ED: Hello? Mr Devers?

DON: The doorstep. Just leave it on the doorstep. Please. Thank you. Thank you very much. I appreciate that. Nice work.

ED: Oh, sorry, I'm not a delivery…I'm Ed. Ryan. Ed Ryan.
(Waits for a response)
We have a meeting. You and I. I get to…we're supposed to meet. You and I.

(On this, a hand reaches for the lever and the recliner strains to the upright position. We hear two claps and a lamp turns on, revealing DON, *mid-fifties. He sits there, blinking at the light.)*

(On his recliner, we see scores of yellow Post-it notes, stuck along both sides of the backrest like tiny wings.)

ED: My wife, Sarah, she set this up. As a birthday gift.
I'm a fan.
Of yours.
Huge.
Since I was eight.
I'm forty. Now.
Just turned. Thus the gift.
It was scheduled for today. Saturday, January 27th.

(DON *starts searching his Post-it notes, pulling one off then putting it back, moving on to the next one, not finding any record of this. He looks at the door unsure what to do.*)

ED: I could come back little later if that's—I mean, just getting to hear your voice through the door, getting to experience that, it's pretty amazing actually. (*Small beat*) Mr Dev—?

DON: (*Impulsively, despite himself*) Yes! Yes, I've been expecting you. Glad you could make it. One moment. Give me one moment.
(*With a hand on either arm of the chair, he pushes himself up and out. Not easy to do. His knees don't bend much if at all. Nor does his spine. He's incredibly tough though.*)
Be right there.
(*He grips the walker that sits to the side of his chair and starts to the door. He doesn't walk really, it's more of a shuffle, so this takes a while. Perhaps a long while. At various points along his epic journey to the door, he needs a quick break, then continues.*)
Any minute now.
(*Shuffles for a bit*)
(*Chuckles*)
Here I come.
(*Shuffles for a bit.*)
Patience is a virtue.
(*Chuckles*)

(Finally DON reaches the door. He straightens his body to the extent he can, puts on a real big smile and a big personality to match, then lets ED in.)

DON: *(Broadly)* Well hello there! Good to see you. It's good to see you.

(DON thrusts his hand out, but ED can only stare at him, in awe.)

DON: Did you leave your hand at home?

ED: My…?

(ED sees DON's hand now. He shakes.)

ED: Wow, your hand, I'm shaking your hand. I am shaking Don Devers hand. This is, Mr Devers, this is such an honor .

DON: The honor's all mine. And it's Don, call me Don. Come in, come in. Welcome to Chateau Devers.

ED: Thank you.

DON: Make yourself at home.

ED: Thank you so much. I'm so, so excited to be here. Nervous. Wow.

(ED steps into the room, taking it in. DON's recliner is the only piece of furniture in this tiny living room, other than a nightstand positioned to one side of it and a rolly cart on the other.)

(On top of the cart are an insane number of pill bottles, carefully arranged, with several small bottles of Gatorade and plastic cups.)

(On the shelf below sit cans and cans and cans of Pringles potato chips.)

(ED watches DON shuffle back to the recliner, taking in the full extent of his difficulties.)

DON: Post-surgical. The walker. Still strong as a horse. Not from the glue factory, are you?

(He erupts in a boisterous cackle. A beat. Finally, he reaches his chair. He places his hands on either arm of the chair and drops himself into it. It's clearly painful, but he covers it all with charm and humor.)

A little light on the furniture, I know. I'd invite you to sit here... I mean I'm friendly, but not that friendly.

(DON bursts out, cackling again. ED just stands there smiling awkwardly, nowhere to sit. Finally, with no other option, he bends down and takes a seat on the floor.)

DON: Where are my manners? Can I offer you anything? Gatorade? Pringles?

ED: No, no thank you. I'm fine.

DON: Pringles. You kidding?

ED: Really, I don't want to cause you any—

(DON flips a can of Pringles to ED. ED catches the can [or doesn't as the case may be].)

DON: Good hands. *(Or "tough catch")*

ED: Lucky I don't have Don Devers ready to lower the boom on me. Not safe to be a wide receiver over the middle with Don Devers around.

DON: I was never out to injure anyone. *Never.*

ED: Oh, no, of course not, *of course not.* After you tackled them, you'd help them up, you'd ask if they were all right, then tell them the same thing would happen again the next time they entered your territory.

DON: *(Impressed)* That's right.

ED: And with number of tackles you had—well the N F L didn't even keep those stats back then—but I counted, I kept my own tally of your tackles. In your rookie season for instance you had 32 solo tackles and 12 assisted. So that's 44 times that you helped an opponent to his feet. I always thought that was so... honorable.

DON: Thank you.

(He gets his own can of Pringles.)

Please. Enjoy.

(DON and ED each pull the lid and vacuum-sealed top from his Pringles can. They eat a chip. A couple of awkward beats as they just sit there, crunching. Crunching)

DON: Tasty aren't they?

ED: Yes.

DON: And they're good for the brain. Bet you didn't know that?

ED: No, I…

DON: Little known fact.

(Another awkward beat as DON and ED crunch their chips, neither sure what to say next.)

DON: It's good to see you.

ED: It's a real honor. To *meet* you.

DON: *(Covering)* When I say, good to see you. That's a figure of speech. Good to see you. It makes a person feel as if they're a friend. That you've known each other a while. I used to say it to my clients. In my law practice. Even when I was meeting them for the first time. Like you and I are. For the first time.

ED: Of course. I'm sorry, I didn't mean to…

DON: Bet you didn't know I became a lawyer.

ED: I did, actually.

DON: Handful of us in that club. Law school after football. Fred McNeill. Vikings. Steve Young. Niners. Alan Page. Vikings. How 'bout those Vikings, huh? Veritable legal pipeline. I don't practice anymore. Decided it was time. *My* choice. *Mine.* It was my choice.

ED: That's terrific.

DON: They threw me a retirement party. My firm.

ED: That must have been really nice.

(DON *looks for a Post-it note, peels it off the chair.*)

DON: Month, day, and time. Of the retirement party.
And the name of my firm.

(DON *holds it up for* ED *to see.*)

(*Then a moment of self-consciousness off* ED's *look.*)

DON: A few daily reminders is all.

ED: No, of course, I mean, *The Don Devers Post-it Notes*!
Like you had in your locker. The Post-its all over your
locker. I loved that. The inspirational sayings, the
quotes, things to focus on for a particular game. I loved
it so much that I did it too. As a kid. All along the wall
next to my bed I had my own yellow Post-it notes, a
ton of them, like wallpaper practically. I wrote my own
sayings on them, pick-me-ups. And then, then it came.
What you wrote to me. I have it. I've always had it. I
brought it with me, so I could show you.
(*About to dig in to his bag or jacket or bag*)

DON: Are you a reporter?

ED: No. I mean I wish. I work—worked for a retail
company. Internal communications. Intra-office
newsletters. That sort of thing. Was there a long time. It
was a good day job, actually. Benefits.

(DON *just looks at* ED.)

ED: I got laid off. Few months ago.
(*Tiny beat*)
Sportswriting. That's what I'm really trying to do.

DON: Who are you with?

ED: No, no I'm not with a paper or anything. If only.
I mean, I've had few small things printed here or there.

I have a blog.
I keep at it though. Eighteen years and counting.
Though I'm kind of freaked out at the moment, truth
be told.

(ED *waits, hoping* DON *will respond to this. A beat*)

DON: Are you married?

ED: Am I...? Yes, I am.

DON: I used to be married. She died.

ED: I'm very sorry to hear that.

DON: Car crash. Which was my fault. *And don't try to
tell me it wasn't, it was!!* I have it right here.
(*He peels another Post-it from his chair and holds it up.*)
Your wife, is she living?

ED: Uh, yes, she's...living.

DON: Good. Good man. I'm happy for you.

ED: Thank you.
We're expecting our first child, actually.

DON: There you go.

ED: I don't know, it's...I grew up without a father,
same with you I know, so I don't really... Kinda scared
I won't know how to do it. Or what it means even. Was
it like that for you?

DON: It's hard.

ED: Yeah?

DON: Loving someone more than yourself. Don't let
anyone tell you that's easy. It's the hardest thing there
is.
(*Tiny beat*)
Have you picked a name for her yet? Your daughter.

ED: No. And it's a boy. Oh boy.

(DON *peers at* ED.)

DON: She sent you here, did she send you here?

ED: Sent? No, this was a birthday gift. The most amazing—

DON: Stephanie sent you here?

ED: Stephanie? No, *no*. I mean, I don't even know who that is. Who's Stephanie?

DON: *My daughter. My daughter, Stephanie.* You're the one who knocked her up. Is that you?

ED: Me? No, I'm married.

DON: Darn right you are. Didn't seem to stop you though.

ED: To Sarah, my wife's name is—

DON: She thinks you can change my mind, is that it?

ED: Don, Mr Devers, I think you're misunderstand—

(*Suddenly* DON *grabs his walker and launches it at* ED. *It narrowly misses him.*)

DON: You tell her to stay away from here! Stay away from this house! Don't call, don't come by, don't send a proxy or a messenger. Did she think I would forget, is that it?! Well I won't!
(*He peels off another Post-it note.*)
I have it right here. Tell her I have it right here! Tell her!
(*He slams a Gatorade bottle off his cart.*)

ED: Mr Devers, I apologize if I did anything to—

DON: *TELL HER!!*

ED: I will, I'll tell her, I'm sorry!
(*He dashes to escape.*)

Scene 2

(ED, completely unnerved, heart racing, meets a very pregnant STEPHANIE on the street.)

STEPHANIE: What happened? What's wrong?!

ED: *He thought I got you pregnant, that you sent me!*

STEPHANIE: Did you mention me, *I told you not to mention me!*

ED: I didn't.

STEPHANIE: *That was the one thing we went over!* Don't mention you talked to me, that you met me, that you even know who I am!

ED: I didn't mention! No mention! I just said I'm having a boy and he launched his walker at my head!

STEPHANIE: Let's just calm the fuck down here! You calm down, I'll calm down, this little fucking alien inside me will calm down! Calm the fuck down little alien!

(ED and STEPHANIE try to calm down. They breathe. Breathe)

STEPHANIE: Calm?

ED: No. You?

STEPHANIE: Fuck no. I don't do calm.

ED: I'm such an idiot. It doesn't work to meet your heros in real life. I don't need to see him like this.

STEPHANIE: Oh was that hard for you?

ED: I'm sorry, he's your father, I'm sure it must be…

STEPHANIE: You don't know shit about what it must be. He played nine years in the N F L smashing into people. I mean, what do you expect?

ED: I don't know!

STEPHANIE: Okay. Okay. It's all right, it's all good.
He just got a little confused, honest mistake. I set up
two visits so we've still got tomorrow. You'll go back
tomorrow.

ED: With what, a helmet and pads?

STEPHANIE: I'll get you a suit of fucking armor if I need
to.

ED: I can't believe I'm saying this, but maybe I should
leave. Maybe I should go back to the airport and fly
standby or something.

STEPHANIE: No, no, no. No airport. You are not leaving.
You're going back, you have to go back.

ED: Don't you think I want to? My god, your father has
meant more to me than you can possibly—

STEPHANIE: Your dad died when you were six, hard
childhood, blah, blah, etc. etc.

ED: Wow.

STEPHANIE: Empathy. Not my strong suit.

ED: Apparently.

STEPHANIE: Hey, your wife put a lot of work into this.
Sent me like a thousand-and-one emails to set this up.

ED: He scared the heck out of me.
But still…it was him. It was still him. I sat there on the
floor and I felt like, like a little boy. I wanted to tell him
everything then hear what he'd say. Especially after
I showed him the note. Which I didn't do. *Oh shoot, I
didn't get to show him the note.*

STEPHANIE: So…tomorrow.

ED: Tomorrow. Okay. Yes. I'll show him the note
tomorrow.

STEPHANIE: There you go. Day two with your hero,
here you come.

(Jangles her keys)
Well don't just stand there. Come on, I'll drive you
back to your hotel.

(ED and STEPHANIE exit.)

Scene 3

(DON's condo. Late night. Chair reclined. Only his tube-socked feet sticking out. It seems like he might be asleep until, after a beat, his hand reaches for the lever and he jams the chair upright. Frustration)

(He claps the lamp on. He grabs one of his pill bottles and shakes two out. Takes them. He decides to take one more. Then closes the bottle, claps the light off, and reclines again.)

(A beat. Two beats)

(The chair flies upright again. Lamp clapped on again. He sits there a moment. There's something flickering, on and off in his brain, barely whispering to him. He listens deeply, desperate to hear the voice inside.)

(Suddenly he grabs his Post-it note pad and quickly scrawls a sentence. When he's done, he looks at what he's written, baffled.)

DON: What does this mean?

(Frustrated, DON peels the Post-it off and crumples it. Then stops and un-crumples it, looking at it again. He decides to stick it on his chair after all, giving it a place with the others.)

(He reaches for another pill bottle. He starts to open it then slams it down. He turns to his night table, opens the drawer, and reaches inside.)

(He pulls out a hand-held taser.)

(He claps off the lamp and reclines. In the dark, we hear a few big breaths to brace himself, then the fizzling sound of

electric current. He is holding the taser to his body, tasing himself unconscious.)

(His body jerks violently, five maybe six seconds, until... silence.)

Scene 4

(Lights come up on DON, *the next morning. Asleep in his chair. The doorbell rings.* ED *at the door.)*

DON: The doorstep. Just leave it on the doorstep. Please. Thank you. Thank you very much. I appreciate that. Nice work.

ED: Mr Devers, it's me. Ed. Ryan. Ed Ryan. I'm ba-ack. Today, Sunday, January 28th, 1pm. Our second scheduled time together. That's what your daughter told me. Your daughter...*Stephanie.*

(And up flies the recliner.)

ED: I do know her. I want to be honest with you. But just to be clear, I am not, *I am not* the guy who, you know...impregnated her. Your daughter.

*(*DON *takes the taser off his chair and reaches for his walker. He pulls himself up. Pain. He starts his shuffle to the door.)*

ED: I want to be very clear about that. I just met her. She was the one my wife, my wife *Sarah,* contacted. To arrange this.
I really hope you let me in. There's something I really, really need to show you.

*(*ED *leaves it at that, waits.* DON *continues to the door. Eventually reaches it.* ED *steps into the apartment.)*

ED: Mr Devers, Don, thank you—

*(*DON *puts the taser to* ED.*)*

DON: On your knees.

ED: Is that—

DON: It's a taser. On your knees.

(ED *goes to his knees.*)

ED: Mr Devers, please.

DON: I do apologize, this is certainly no way to treat
a guest, but I told you. No more. Understand? I don't
care what my daughter told you, no more nurses.
You're fired.
And I'm sorry about your chin.

ED: Don, I'm not, I'm not a nurse, I'm a fan, of yours, I
swear I'll leave you alone as soon as I…

(ED, *still at taser-point, quickly reaches to his pocket and
pulls out a yellow Post-it note, laminated for preservation.*)

DON: What is that? *Tell me what that is!*

ED: When I was a kid, I wrote to you, and you, you
sent me this.

(ED *holds it out.* DON *stares. He takes the Post-it with one
hand, keeping the taser on* ED *with the other.* DON *reads the
Post-it. It strikes him, profoundly.*)

ED: I watched you every Sunday. Fierce, you were so
fierce. But at the same time, like really polite and really
smart. And then I found out your father died when
you were a kid, like me, my father died when I was six,
so I wrote to you and told you about it. And how bad
things got. How we had nothing. How poor I was, how
badly I got bullied, how scared I was to go to school.
But I thought, you, if I could just be like you, so I wrote
to you to tell you how much I wished I could just be
like you. And then, and then you sent me that. That
Post-it note. Told me you peeled it right off your locker
and sent to me.
"Your greatest moment is yet to come."

That…it meant everything to me. Coming from you. It saved my life, it really did. Because I swear I was ready to…

"Your greatest moment is yet to come."

And then Sarah found you, somehow she found you and I thought, holy cow, I can give him the note, show him the impact it's had on me. Except now, now I realize that's not why I wanted to show it to you. I realize I wanted to show it to you because—I don't believe it anymore, that my greatest moment is yet to come. For the first time in my life I don't believe it. And now, I'm lost. I am lost and this is not the time to be lost because I am about to be a father, and I'm unemployed, and…and so here I am, on one of the truly most exciting days of my life, and I realize that the thing I want, the thing I want most in meeting you…is your help. So maybe, maybe I can still believe that note.

(Pause)

DON: Top right.

ED: Top…?

DON: The chair. Top right sticky. The crumpled one. Bring it here.

(ED rises. He steps very gingerly around DON and goes to the chair.)

ED: This one?

DON: Yes.

(ED pulls it off and brings it over to DON.)

DON: Read it.

(ED reads it to himself first. Looks up. DON nods meaningfully.)

ED: I don't…

DON: Say it.

ED: He's the one.

DON: It came to me. Last night. So I wrote it down. He's. The. One. I understand now. You. It means you.

ED: Me?

DON: You. You're the one.

ED: I'm not sure I…

DON: You're going to come here. This week. All week through Sunday. Superbowl Sunday.

ED: Are you…are you saying *you want to watch the Superbowl with me?*

DON: And document it. Our week together. The Superbowl. All of it.

ED: Document it? Like write a piece? About you?

DON: Yes sir.

ED: With access to you? For a week? That's what you're saying to me, *is that what you're saying to me?*

DON: Video too. It'll be multimedia.

ED: And can I, you'll let me make it…public? Like, send it around? Like…to be seen?

DON: That's the idea. For people to see.
That sound okay to you?

ED: Sound…okay? *Are you kidding?* This is. This is way beyond what I could ever hope…I knew it. I knew meeting you would…thank you. *Thank you.*

(DON *shuffles to his chair. He grabs his Post-it pad and writes.*)

DON: I've got you down now. So I'll know it's you when you come back.
(*He places the sticky in a prime spot on his chair. Then he lowers himself into his chair, looks at* ED.)

You're the one.

ED: I am, I totally am, I'm the one. And you, you totally picked right. I won't let you down. I swear.

Scene 5

(ED *with* STEPHANIE, *mid-report. She shoves him hard, ecstatic.*)

STEPHANIE: Holy shit, holy fucking shit! He really said that?

ED: He really said that.

STEPHANIE: Ah! I'm so happy with you right now, *I could stuff you inside my placenta!*

(Off ED's *look:)*

STEPHANIE: I know, I know, this is how I talk, *but do you not understand what's happened here?*
My father doesn't see anyone anymore. No one. Refuses to see a doctor, a physical therapist, a visiting nurse, a friend, *me*, especially me, no one. And I didn't tell him you were coming by the way, that was a lie, you might have guessed that by now, he doesn't take my calls, or emails, or letters, nothing, so I just threw you in there, my bad, but now, now there's at least someone, one person he'll see.

ED: Me!

STEPHANIE: *You.* And that, that is going to make all the difference. I know it. I know it will.

ED: I'm the one!

(STEPHANIE *shoves* ED *hard again.*)

STEPHANIE: *This is exactly what I hoped would happen!*

ED: Oh my god, I better call Sarah. Shoot, shoot I can't leave her home for a week.

STEPHANIE: Then fly her out here.

ED: We can't afford that.

STEPHANIE: Then let me buy it. I'll buy her ticket.

ED: Are you serious?

STEPHANIE: You're seeing my father tomorrow. Nothing, *nothing's* getting in the way of that. No, I'll book her ass on a flight. Today. Right the fuck now. *(She pulls out her phone to make a flight, exits as she does.)*

Scene 6

(ED's hotel room, later. SARAH enters, suitcase in tow. She's pregnant and showing, mid-second trimester.)

(She sees him and drops the suitcase, goes to him, they hug.)

SARAH: Oh my God, Ed.

ED: Don Devers. Don. Devers.

SARAH: *I'm so, so happy for you.*

ED: I mean, when you got me this, this gift, which ranks very, very high in the gift category, I thought, okay, maybe I'll get to spend an hour with him then I'll go home and blog about it on my blog that no one reads, but then this, this happens. And it is way beyond what I could ever…I mean, Don's not a star, not too many people remember who he is. And lord knows no one knows who the hell I am. But still. Someone might really be interested in this. It could be a full-on feature article with accompanying video and everything.

SARAH: Or even a book.

ED: A book?

SARAH: Like a *Tuesdays with Morrie* sort of thing.

ED: Is that a joke? Tuesdays with Morrie was a best-seller.

SARAH: Can you imagine?

ED: It spent two hundred weeks on the best seller list. Sold over fourteen million copies.

SARAH: Which might be just enough to pay our back rent.

(ED *stung.*)

SARAH: I was joking. It was a joke. Ed, come on.

ED: I know how behind we are. You think I don't know that?

SARAH: I know, I know you do.

ED: I've tried, I've tried to find something else, you know I tried.

SARAH: Of course, of course I do.

ED: I 've tried really effin' hard. I mean this economy, and I'm a forty, and they're all looking for kids who can afford to take these paltry freelance jobs, which is all there is, which pay peanuts, not nearly enough for rent, or health insurance, or to support a child on the way.

SARAH: I know.

ED: I know we're in trouble, I know, and I'm trying, I'm trying really effin' hard.

SARAH: I know you are. And I know how unsettled it's made you. Which we haven't talked about. I mean, what *have* we talked about lately? I assume because, well, things are tense. But I see you. Feel you. In the apartment. Stalking around. Not even volunteering at the high school anymore, doing their stats. You love that.

ED: I'm not hanging around the high school anymore because I don't have a job and I don't want to be that guy *with no job* who hangs around the high school doing their stats!

SARAH: Hey, come on. Let's not do this. Something amazing happened that just might change everything.

ED: Is that why you came? You're afraid I'll mess it up?

SARAH: Is that an accusation?

ED: Is it true?

SARAH: My God, will you please…I came to support you so you can do this and not have you worry about your pregnant wife home alone. Okay? Are *you* afraid you'll mess it up?

(ED *says nothing.*)

SARAH: You won't.

ED: How do you know?

SARAH: Because…because from the day we met, I've watched you, watched you trying. And doing so with integrity, and honor. Not even "effin" cursing when you're upset.

(*Perhaps* ED *smiles.*)

SARAH: And never, never giving up. And that's the guy I fell in love with. The total antidote to what I grew up with, to the jerk who ran out on my mother and me. Because you are the guy who doesn't disappear. Who sticks to it, who tries and tries and tries to become the man he wants to be. The man I knows he can be.

(*A beat*)

ED: What if this meant you could stop freelancing.

SARAH: But oh how I'd miss my low end graphic design gigs which barely pay our groceries.

(ED *and* SARAH *smile.*)

SARAH: Though I've got one this week. A gig.

ED: You do?

SARAH: Stephanie hired me.

ED: She hired you?

SARAH: Paying me pretty well actually.

ED: What does she even do, is she some kind of dominatrix or something?

SARAH: She's an accountant. Works from home. I'm helping her redo her logo. And that's not all, she invited us to stay with her. She has an extra room. So we don't even need to pay for the hotel.

ED: Sarah, I don't know, that woman, I mean we don't even really know her, and you're going to work for her, we're going to live with her?

SARAH: I do know her.

ED: From a thousand-and-one emails?

SARAH: It feels like it took that many. To convince her to let you see her dad. At least at first. But then it continued, the emails. We kind of, I don't know, hit it off. And I have to say, it's been a really nice thing for me. To have someone to talk to. Who's in my situation. Who understands. Who's totally different from the women in the "Expectant mother's group".

ED: She is certainly different from them.

SARAH: Uck. They're all so smug.

ED: Hippy-dippy.

SARAH: New-agey.

ED: Posting all their pictures.

SARAH: Like each one of them is the first woman in the universe to ever have a baby.

ED & SARAH: *Which if they even just looked around the room…*
(*They chuckle at their routine. Tension diffused. Small beat.*)

ED: Don refuses to see her. Did you know that? His own daughter.

SARAH: Between us? She slept with a football player. Which was always forbidden. And this was a married one, which she didn't know, he lied about it. And he wants nothing to do with the baby. Which is just fine with Stephanie. Her father, though, he's pretty upset about the whole thing. Okay?

ED: Will you at least cover the baby's ears when you're with her?

(SARAH *smiles. Small beat*)

ED: It's incredible, right?

SARAH: Yes.

ED: This could finally be a break, the start of something.

SARAH: I hope so. (*Her belly*) He hopes so—woh, woh, on cue, hold on.

(SARAH *takes* ED's *hand, places it on her belly.*)

SARAH: You feel that?

ED: Wow, what was that?

SARAH: His elbow I think.

ED: His elbow.
(*Moved*)
Our boy has an elbow.
(*A beat*)
You think it's still true?

SARAH: I know it is.
Your greatest moment is yet to come.

Scene 7

(Lights up on ED. *He's ready. Super ready. A small note book in his hand, a pencil behind his ear. In his other hand, a cheap folding chair. Big breath, big breath, okay. Here we go. He rings the doorbell.)*

(Lights up on DON. *He's already up and out of his chair. He has several Post-it notes stuck along his sleeve. He re-checks them then calls out.)*

DON: It's open. Enter. Entre vous. Come on in.

*(*ED *enters, cautiously.)*

ED: Hi.

DON: *(Points)* Ed.

ED: That's right. So you, you remember who I am, right?

DON: Yes, yes I do.
(Pulls one of the Post-it notes off his arm)
Got it right here. Come in. Come in, come in, come in.

ED: Just to be clear, you know I'm not your nurse, right? And I didn't, your daughter and I, we've had no physical contact whatsoever.

DON: There's Pringles and Gatorade for breakfast today. Right there on the table if you're hungry. Pringles to the left, Gatorade to the right. Help yourself then we'll get started.

ED: Fantastic. Holy cow. He we go. This is it.
(He pulls out his notes.)

DON: Notes? Jeez, I thought I was one with brain damage. C T E. Chronic Traumatic Encephalopathy. The orange goop they keep finding in our brains after we're dead? Those of us who made a living using our heads as battering rams. Hey, here's one for you.

In what way are football players and prostitutes the same?
(Barely waiting for a response)
We both ruin our bodies for the pleasure of strangers.
(He cracks up. Then stops)
So, how do we do this? Our little project, our little *Tuesdays with Morrie* thing.

ED: You see, that book sold over—

DON: We should start with a title. Not *A Week with Don*, not that. We need something better, more accurate. How about *D-day with Don*? *Disaster with Don*? *Dog Days with Don*? It should be alliterative I think. What do you think? Maybe a title isn't important for now. Let's leave the title and just get started. Pringles and Gatorade on the table if you're hungry. Pringles to the left, Gatorade to the right.

ED: Thank y—

DON: And right there are my files. Medical. The surgeries, medications, all of it. Take them. Go ahead. For your perusal. Perusal, which means careful consideration by the way. Most people use that word incorrectly. They think it means to take a quick glance or skim, but it does not. In my law practice, I'd tell a client I perused the documents and they'd get all, then I'd enjoy correcting them. I'm talking fast, am I talking fast? I'm a tad nervous I suppose. Feeling a bit exposed. Maybe more than a bit.

ED: That's perfectly—

DON: Plus I went over dosage on the Provigil. And the Aricept. And the Adderall. Wanted to be as sharp as possible, nice and ready for this. Hey, did you know they're popping Adderall now as a performance enhancer?

ED: I read about that.

DON: More energy, definitely more energy. More focus. Temporary of course. And it's a sleep inhibitor. Is it ever. So then the cycle. Adderall or Provigil to get up, stay up, then painkillers and narcotics to bring you back down so you can sleep. Unless you can't sleep, which I can't, then you'll need even more Adderall the next day and later more narcotics to bring you back down. Adderal-provigil-narcotics, adderal-provigil-narcotics, vicious cycle, wow, I'm going a mile a minute aren't I? The brain cells are really firing this morning. Alright, let's strike while the iron's hot. Sit down have a Pringle, then you can get right to it. Fire away.

ED: Okay, okay. Oh my god. Here we go.

(Maybe ED *unfolds his chair and sits.* DON *remains standing.)*

DON: I gave you classic flavor. I also have Tangy Buffalo Wing. Three times the sodium if you want that. Good for the brain. Okay, fire away. The tough questions. Whatever you want to ask me. Shoot.

ED: *(Fired up)* Okay. My first question. Here it comes. If there was one thing, and one thing only, you could say to the young players out there—what would it be?

DON: Easy. Don't play football you dimwit.
(He cracks up, then serious to ED*)*
You know, they like to say football is a contact sport. That is incorrect. It is not a contact sport, it is a collision sport. Collision. Even the smallest hit, two linemen coming together, thirty to a hundred g's of force. That's a car crash, twenty miles per hour. A player has about a thousand of those a season. A thousand car crashes each and every year he plays.

ED: Oh my G—

DON: And the guys just retiring you ask? What would I tell them? It gets worse. That's what I'd tell them. It gets worse. Sometimes very quickly. Precipitous. P-r-e-c-i-p-i-t-o-u-s. Pre-cipitous. Boom. Spelling bee. Okay, what else? Shoot. Come on, come on. Dig deep.

ED: Do you talk to any other players? Ones going through, like what you are?

DON: Talk? No. Not talk. Read though. A wealth of information. Ideas. Operating instructions. Learned about the taser, for instance.

(Chuckles)

I should be their national spokesman. "In excruciating pain? Sleep in a recliner because you can't make it in and out of your own bed? So hopped up on your twenty-plus daily medications you can't sleep? Well try this simple method to bring on the sandman: sit back, relax, and zap yourself unconscious."

ED: That's why you…you use the taser on yourself?

DON: Only thing that works.

ED: Jesus, that's horrible.

(DON's boisterous laugh. Stops on a dime. Serious)

DON: I have to pee.

ED: Oh. Okay. Uhm, do you like, uh…need help to the…?

DON: Oh boy, oh boy, oh boy. Here we go, I wanted to show you this. I did. Except now I'm nervous. I am nervous. I'm going to admit that to you. Feeling a bit exposed. More than a bit. You know who James Dean is? His first film. *Rebel Without a Cause.* One of my favorites. They say he was on the film set, his first day, and he was so nervous he wasn't sure he could even go through with it. So he decided he needed to do something to just blast those nerves away. They're outside, setting up for a shot, and right there, in front of everyone, Dean pulls his pants down and urinates. Figured he'd embarrass himself so badly that nothing he could do from then on could possibly match it. And his nerves went away.

ED: Don, Don, oh boy, okay, please, you really don't have to…

DON: Already have.
(*He cackles. Then serious. He holds onto the walker with one hand and starts to scoot down his track pants with the other.*)

ED: Uh…Don?

(DON *gets his pants down, revealing the adult diaper he wears underneath.*)

DON: Tada.

(DON *tears off the wet diaper, standing there exposed. [The extent of his nudity can obviously be adjusted as one sees fit. He can go behind a piece of furniture to pull off the diaper, thus exposing nothing, but still vividly showing* ED *the reality of his situation.] He proceeds to open the drawer of his side table and pull out a ziplock bag. He puts the diaper into it, seals it, then drops it in the nearby garbage. He reaches into the drawer and grabs a fresh diaper. He un-velcros it and puts it on. Not easy given how stiff he is. Once he manages to get it on, he uses one hand to pull his track pants back up. By the time he's done, he's utterly exhausted.*)

DON: (*Spent, sober*) That's probably enough for today.

(ED *nods, head down, mortified. He starts off.*)

DON: Don't forget your breakfast.

ED: That's…

DON: Please, what kind of host would I be?

(ED *turns, collects the Pringles and Gatorade, and rushes out.*)

Scene 8

(SARAH *and* STEPHANIE *sit in* STEPHANIE's *condo, their pregnant bellies protruding—comrades in pregnancy. [Note: it's important their pregnant bellies are visible to the audience—a major visual of their common situation, bonding, anxiety, life-bringing. They should not be sitting behind a table or anything that obscures them].)*

(On the table behind them [or to the side] sits a tablet, maybe a variety of printouts, envelops, etc. A work session was in progress though not at the moment.)

(At the moment, they're facing each other, pinched faces, straining mightily, big physical discomfort. They're doing Kegels.)

(After several seconds of intense effort, STEPHANIE counts down from five on her fingers. At zero, they exhale, releasing their clenching. They try to catch their breath.)

SARAH: Are these really necessary?

STEPHANIE: Strong pelvic floor muscles combat post-birth incontinence. You like peeing yourself?

SARAH: Not particularly.

STEPHANIE: And Kegels keep your cunt muscles tight, which I'm sure your husband will appreciate.

SARAH: Did you…did you just say the C-word?

STEPHANIE: No, of course, I didn't say "the C-word". I said cunt.

SARAH: *Oh my god, I'm so happy I'm here.*

STEPHANIE: So what do you call yours?

SARAH: What? No.

STEPHANIE: Come on.

SARAH: You're going to laugh.

STEPHANIE: I won't.

SARAH: You will.

STEPHANIE: Come on, spit it out.

SARAH: *(Barely audible)* Hoo-hah.

STEPHANIE: What?

SARAH: *Hoo-hah, I call it a hoo-hah.*

(STEPHANIE cracks up.)

SARAH: You see?

STEPHANIE: No, no, sorry. It's good, it's good. I learned something new about you.

SARAH: Well, that's the last time I—

STEPHANIE: What? Tell me a ridiculous name for your vagina?

SARAH: I'm getting back to work.
(She grabs her tablet.)

STEPHANIE: I'm sorry. You see? This is why I have no friends, why I'm a single mother, why I'm destined to die alone.

SARAH: I hope you don't really feel that way.

STEPHANIE: It's a fact. It's why you're the first person in a very long time to come inside this house without a shoe box full of tax receipts. Come on, don't be mad. More Kegels?

(SARAH smiles.)

SARAH: Do you want to see what I have so far?

STEPHANIE: Hell yeah.

(SARAH, about to show STEPHANIE the tablet, hesitates.)

SARAH: It's just a first draft, I can put the logo, everything back the—

STEPHANIE: Blah, blah, disclaimer, disclaimer, bullshit, bullshit.

SARAH: I've never been good as presenting my work. Probably why things have never—

STEPHANIE: Let's see it.

(SARAH *turns the tablet to* STEPHANIE. *A beat as* STEPHANIE *examines the work.*)

SARAH: You don't like it.

STEPHANIE: No, it's not that. It's just—I think I didn't really know what I wanted. Until you showed me. I love it.

(SARAH *smiles, enormously pleased.*)

(ED *enters with a file in his hands.*)

SARAH: How'd it go?

STEPHANIE: How is he, how'd it go?

ED: He…shared some things with me.

STEPHANIE: Oh shit. Like what?

(ED *opens the file. Reads it to* SARAH.)

ED: Posterior Cervical Laminectomy at C6-7 with Removal of Hard Disc Compressing C-7 Nerve Root. Anterior cervical discectomy and fusion at C6-7 and C7-1, utilizing bone-bank bone. *Lower back*: Bilateral L4-5 disc removal followed by mini Knodt rod fusion at the L4-5 level. *Lower back*: Exploration, Removal of Knodt rods. Laminectomy, Discectomy at L5-S1. Right L5-S1 Foraminotomy. Bilateral Lateral L4-5, L5-S1 Fusion. Left Iliac crest Cortical Cancellous Bone Grafting. Insertion of EBI Bone Stimulator. *Lower back*: Removal of Retained EBI Bone Stimulator and Battery. *Lower back*: Decompressive Lumbar Laminectomy of L3-4 with interbody fusion, 4 screws inserted, L3-4. *Left Hip*: Left Primary cementless total hip arthroplasty. *Right Hip*: Right Primary cementless total hip arthroplasty. *Neck*: Cervical discectomy at C4-5.

SARAH: Jesus.

ED: Jesus has nothing on him. Given the choice
between a crucifixion and *this* list?
It says his most recent surgery gave him nerve damage.
Something called "drop foot".

STEPHANIE: It means he can't lift the front part of
his feet, so they drag. Might be fixable with another
surgery.

ED: I can't do this, Sarah, not like this.

SARAH: Ed.

ED: I can't.

SARAH: This is your chance. Our chance.

ED: I will not chronicle his pain and profit from it.

STEPHANIE: Then don't. Help him.

ED: Why don't you? You're his daughter.

STEPHANIE: You pussy.

SARAH: Stephanie.

STEPHANIE: He's just scared "Oh my God, this is so
hard". For fuck's sake, what kind of journalist do you
expect to be if you're freaked out by a little discomfort.

ED: Obviously not a successful one.

SARAH: Ed please, please don't do that yourself.

STEPHANIE: He's isolated. And isolation equals death.
That's what happens to people. You isolate yourself
and you decline. Rapidly. But he's talking to you. He's
giving you materials, his files, he's sharing himself
with you.

ED: Do you really want me to write about how terrible
things are for him? In excruciating, specific, personal
detail? Make that public? Show it around?

STEPHANIE: I don't care. I don't care what it says, I don't care if it becomes public, and I don't care if it's just an entry in your little pink diary. I. Don't. Care. What I care about is that he talks to someone. And that maybe talking to someone, having some human contact with someone who believes in him, who worships him, will help him rejoin the world, see people again, take care of himself again. Jesus Christ, if you're so damn afraid of being self-serving, *then don't be*. Don't want to take? Then *give*. Give something back to him. *For everything he's done for you.*

(STEPHANIE *wants to get up and storm off, but she can't get out of her chair.* SARAH *gives* ED *a look.*)

(*He goes and helps* STEPHANIE *to her feet. They stand face to face, eyeball to eyeball.*)

STEPHANIE: *It's men who should get pregnant!*

(STEPHANIE *storms off now, as previously intended. A beat. Then* ED *starts to laugh.*)

SARAH: Ed, it's not funny.

ED: No, I'm laughing because she's right. She's totally right.

SARAH: If only.

ED: I mean about giving back. That is totally it. Of course it is. What I write, the time we spend together, it'll be about helping Don, not the other way around. That's what this should be, my God of course it is. That's how I can do this. In a way that would be… honorable. As honorable as the man himself is. What do you think?

SARAH: I think the man who's writing about him is pretty darn honorable too.

(*A J F K impersonation*)

Ask not what your hero can do for you, but what you can do for your hero.

ED: Exactly.

(ED *and* SARAH *smile. She sees something in his look.*)

SARAH: What?

ED: I don't know. It might also be good practice for me.

SARAH: How do you mean?

ED: That's what's required of me, isn't it? As a father. Thinking of someone else before myself? (*An idea*) For instance, are you hungry?

SARAH: Oh my God, always.

ED: Close your eyes.

SARAH: What? Why?

ED: I have something for you. Go ahead.

(SARAH *closes her eyes, anxiously anticipating.*)

SARAH: What is it?

(ED *pulls out the can of Pringles.*)

ED: Open your mouth.

(SARAH *does.* ED *gently places a Pringle in her mouth. All the salt, the fat, the sinful guilty pleasure.*)

SARAH: Oh. My. God.
(*She opens her eyes.*)

ED: Another?

SARAH: Oh yes.

(ED *takes out another chip. This time he puts one end in his mouth and leans in to* SARAH. *They bite from each side, which ends in a kiss.*)

SARAH: Wow, who are you and what have you done with my husband?

(ED *recoils, stung.*)

SARAH: No, no sorry. I didn't mean it like that, I meant it as a good thing.

ED: Okay.

SARAH: I wasn't trying to push you away, I just... Come on, feed me another, just like that.

(ED *puts the can down.*)

SARAH: Ed.

ED: It's okay. Really. I'm just going to stand back and watch you enjoy them.

(SARAH *hesitates. Then she takes a chip.* ED *and* SARAH *look at one another. Forced smiles*)

Scene 9

(DON *sits in his chair, awake, his eyes bloodshot, not having slept all night.* ED *rings the doorbell.* DON *looks at the door, unsure. The doorbell again.*)

ED: Hi Don. It's me, Ed. Maybe you left the door open for me again? I'm just going to come in, okay? I'm coming in...
(*He steps into the apartment, excited. He carries a plastic food bag.*)
Morning!

(DON *nods, smiles.*)

ED: I brought you some breakfast.
(*Meaningfully*)
...egg salad sandwich on whole wheat. And cranberry juice. See?

(ED *waits, expecting a big reaction.*)

ED: Egg salad sandwich on whole wheat! And cranberry juice!

(DON *watches* ED *attentively*)

Your pregame meal!

(Still not the response ED's *looking for)*

ED: You ate it before every game. It's what I ate too. Before school. To be like you. Actually before I learned what you ate, I ate crap. My mother, after my dad died, she let me buy whatever I wanted, as long as it was cheap. All that mattered. Count Chocula, Frankenberry, Captain Crunch, Cookie Crisp. I got pretty fat. A fatherless fat kid. Who also had a stutter. I kid you not. A bad one. A fatherless fat kid with a stutter. Not a fun way to go through school. Anyway, what I'm trying say is that I started to eat what you ate and it helped, see? So I brought this for you. I know you like your Pringles, but maybe a change of pace, something from back in the day. Something, you know, a little…healthier.

(He puts the bag on DON's *sidetable.)*

DON: If you're the new nurse, get out.

ED: Are you…? Don, Don, it's me. Ed.

DON: You might want to talk to the last nurse that didn't leave when I asked him to.

ED: Don, Don, Post-it note, upper right on the top most—check it. Please.

(DON slowly turns, looks at the Post-it, then turns back to ED. Recognition. He's got it now.)

DON: Ed.

ED: That's right.
You look like you didn't sleep much. Maybe the Adderall? You said yesterday you went over your dosage.

DON: Why did I do that, I should not have done that.

ED: You just wanted to be up. Prepared. That's all. To show me, you know…what you showed me. Anyway, I was doing a little research, you know, and it turns out, "dropfoot", there's actually some things you can do.

DON: No. No more surgeries.

ED: Well, that was just one option.

DON: No one cuts into this body ever again.

ED: The thing is, though, if there was something you could do, if you could walk a little better, get to the bathroom a little faster, you wouldn't have to, you know…James Dean it. I mean, my God you've done so much for me, I just want to give something back to you.

DON: You are.

ED: I am?

DON: You're the one.

ED: I have to say, the way you say that…is there something I don't know?

(DON *looks at* ED *a beat.*)

DON: I suppose it's time.

(DON *pulls a Post-it from the chair and hands it to* ED.)

DON: Read it.

ED: He's the one. You showed me—

DON: Now the back.

(ED *turns the Post-it over.*)

ED: Ed Ryan is the one. On Sunday, Ed and I will watch the Superbowl together. At halftime Ed will take video. He will record me as I…as I commit the act of suicide.

(*A small beat then* DON *cracks up.*)

DON: My apologies, my apologies. Though Morrie does die at end.

ED: He doesn't kill himself and have it recorded.

DON: Be a better book if he did.

ED: I'm glad you're joking.

DON: I'm not.

ED: You wouldn't really do this.

DON: Oh, I most certainly will.
(*Chuckles*)
You said you wanted to help.

ED: You don't mean it.

DON: I do.

ED: *No you don't.* You wouldn't do that. And you wouldn't ask me to help you.

DON: No, not help help. Just record. Then post it. Online. At halftime. Of the Superbowl.

ED: (*Jumping up*) I'm calling Stephanie, *I'm calling Stephanie right now*—

DON: No. *No.*

ED: She's your daughter.

DON: She'll come here. *She cannot come here!*

ED: *Don*—

DON: You're married Ed.

ED: *So?*

DON: *So I was married.* She died.

ED: I know, I'm very—

DON: I rammed her. Her head.

ED: You...?

DON: Against a wall. I killed her.

ED: It was a car accident.

DON: *I smashed her head against the wall!*
She was a good driver. She was always a good driver.
Driving along, maybe she was dizzy, or a headache, or
confusion. That can happen. Even weeks later that can
happen.

ED: You think she had a concussion?

DON: She was a good driver.

ED: Is that…that's why you won't see Stephanie?
You're afraid you'll do something? You're afraid you'll
hurt her? Or…or the baby?

DON: Mood swings. Impulsive behavior. It gets worse.
Suddenly. *Precipitously.*

ED: But…

DON: *That's what happens.* We do things. Out of
character. To the ones we love. *All of us.*
(A beat. Suddenly he cracks up.)
And you thought today would be about improving my
nutrition.

*(ED says nothing, utterly lost. He stares back down at the
Post-it. Refusing to believe it)*

DON: Ed, you thought spending a week with me and
writing some kind of article would be a break. Right?
Well think about what *this* will do for your career. No
one, no one's gotten what you're about to get.

ED: *(Calmly, getting it straight)* And what you're saying
I'm about to get is the chance to record my childhood
hero killing himself during the Superbowl then post it
on freaking youtube?!

DON: Ed. Listen to me. Listen. You came here. A
messenger. With a message.

ED: *I don't understand what you're talking about.* What message?

(A tiny beat as DON *looks at* ED, *smiles gently.)*

DON: That my greatest moment is *yet* to come.

(Blackout)

END OF ACT ONE

ACT TWO

Scene 1

(SARAH and STEPHANIE sitting in STEPHANIE's condo, belly's protruding. There are papers spread out, Sarah's tablet. They each sit with their feet up, their usual positions, one of the few they're comfortable in. STEPHANIE has her eyes closed as SARAH re-enacts a guided meditation.)

SARAH: *(Super, over-the-top new-agey)* "Your cervix is like a rosebud…"
"Ready to open.
The rosebud opens ever so softly, opens and blossoms.
You open and blossom.
Every contraction opens another petal of your rosebud cervix.
For the rose does not resist. It yields and opens. *You* yield and open.
And blossom."

STEPHANIE: *(Opening her eyes)* Wow.

SARAH: "I hope each of you sees now what is possible. An easier, more comfortable birthing. In a way that most mirrors nature."

STEPHANIE: Please tell me she didn't say that.

SARAH: Oh she did. And the whole class, everyone around me, they were all so profoundly moved by it. Why do I always choose these places? I guess I'm always…I don't know.

STEPHANIE: Hoping?

SARAH: *(Admitting it to herself)* Yeah.
So get this—for our next class our homework is to come back with our own image from nature, to use as our "touchstone visual".

STEPHANIE: An erupting volcano.

SARAH: Oh my god, that's perfect.

STEPHANIE: But you should tell it the same way as her rosebud. "Yes ladies, pushing that precious 8-pound gift from Gaia out your tiny 4-inch cervix, it's like an explosion of the Earth Mother's power. Just think of all that lava spewing out of nature's hole."

SARAH: God, how I wish you were in that class with me.

(SARAH and STEPHANIE go back to work. A beat)

SARAH: *(Head down in her tablet, vulnerable)* I'm going to feel like a failure if I get an epidural.

STEPHANIE: Oh please.

SARAH: I will. Like I'm not strong enough or committed enough to my child to do it naturally.

STEPHANIE: That's crap. The first word out of my mouth will be "Epidural". What's your name ma'am? Epidural. Date of birth? Epidural.
Fuck it, we should all do it the Brazilian way. Just make an appointment, pick the preferred birthday, and have your little fucker cut out. And it's Brazil so they probably get a big 'ol wax job at the same time.

SARAH: All the studies say it's better to deliver though the vaginal canal.

STEPHANIE: Except yours won't be delivered through the vaginal canal, it'll be delivered through the hoo-hah canal.

SARAH: You are so mean.

STEPHANIE: What happens when you grow up around football players. Speaking of which, enough of your hippie dippie shit. Back to my way.

SARAH: No more, please.

STEPHANIE: Kegels a day keeps incontinence away.

SARAH: Whoever invented these was definitely a man.

STEPHANIE: Arnold Kegel, 1948.

(ED bounds in, all purpose and intensity.)

SARAH: Saved!

ED: Lockerroom speeches. There are two basic categories.

STEPHANIE: First you foam at the mouth—

ED: *Please, this isn't a joke.*

(SARAH and STEPHANIE don't comment, both struck by ED's urgency.)

ED: One kind of speech uses the adversity of the past as a motivational tool.
The other uses the promise of a better future.
That's it. Those two. Past and future.
Now here's the thing: I'm going to use both. Both.
So Don sees that this moment right now, right now…is the crucial one.
What do you think?

SARAH: I think it sounds great. Wow Ed.

(ED nods, starts off.)

STEPHANIE: So what happened?

ED: *(Stops)* What do mean?

STEPHANIE: I mean there must have been something that inspired this. Come on, give me something, anything, some tiny shred of hope.

ED: *(Caught, scrambles)* It was…it was…the Superbowl. He was talking about our watching it together and, and…what he was looking forward to about it.

STEPHANIE: Really? There's something he's looking forward to? That's amazing.

ED: I better go. Morning. Seems to be…

STEPHANIE: His best time.

(ED nods, exits quickly. STEPHANIE turns to SARAH.)

STEPHANIE: I am very pleased with your husband right now. Very pleased.

SARAH: It's incredible to see him like this.

STEPHANIE: Did you notice how I fed him the words there? I kind of get it, that kind of relationship finish each other's sentence kinda thing.

SARAH: When he proposed to me, he said, "by myself, I'm just a phrase or a clause. But with you, I'm a complete sentence." That was - I loved that.

STEPHANIE: Is it like that in bed too? Like, "oh, oh, I'm going to…" and then you "finish his sentence"?

SARAH: Not for a while. Quite a while.

STEPHANIE: Ouch.

SARAH: We almost did. The other night. He was feeding me Pringles.

STEPHANIE: Oh yeah, Pringle foreplay.

SARAH: But he gets put off so easily. Which isn't all his fault. Nothing feels comfortable to me right now. My whole body, everything's so tender. So I don't always react, you know, as enthusiastically as I could. And things have been stressful in general. To say the least. But still, he does get put off so easily.

STEPHANIE: Didn't look like it just now.

SARAH: No, it didn't.

STEPHANIE: All fired up. You may get some yet.

SARAH: How about you? Are you— "gettin' some"?

(An "are you kidding?" look from STEPHANIE.)

SARAH: Sorry.

(A beat)

STEPHANIE: I've written about twenty moronic texts to the baby daddy. Which I never sent, of course. "Wanna come over for some free tax advice? " "Come early this year so I can "manage your portfolio." "It's 10:40 and I'm 'EZ'."
And once this little guy comes out? Single mom, working from home, sleep deprived, breast feeding. Fuck it, I don't need a man. I've got Jimmyjane.

SARAH: Amen. If you can't have sex, have food.

STEPHANIE: What? No, that's Jimmy *John's*, the sandwich place. Jimmy*jane* makes vibrators. Ones actually made for women. Not from some male porn fantasy. We'll get you one.

SARAH: Oh, I don't think so…

STEPHANIE: It'll tide you over until things come around. "Something ladies that you control, that you can use, to negotiate those tender spots." I should be their national spokeswoman. Okay, end of rousing speech. You'll get one today.

SARAH: Uh…

Scene 2

(ED mid-speech, giving it his all. DON sits in his chair, lucid, listening. He wears a spiffy blazer over his usual sweatshirt.)

ED: …and then in the final game of the season, you separate your shoulder in the first half. On the

sidelines, they push your arm back in to its socket,
wrap it up, and you do, you go back out there. And
you guys win. And remember, remember what you
said about why you went back in? Remember? Because
you wanted to show the young players on your team
the level of commitment needed to get over that hump.
You see? No matter what the injury was, or the setback,
you always got back in the game. And you always will.
You'll show players everywhere who are struggling
how it's done.

(Speech over. ED *waits anxiously for* DON *to say
something.)*

DON: When I think back to that game, I do realize
something.

ED: *Yeah?* What, what do you realize?

DON: My shoulder was never the same after that.
(He cracks up.)
 I'm sorry, I apologize. It's me. I just don't like
lockerroom speeches. Though you did well. I
commend you. Using both the past and the future. A
high level approach. Most guys just pick one.

ED: You don't like lockerroom speeches?

DON: They're ephemeral. Sure, they might get you all
fired up to get out there, but that kind of emotion only
lasts a few plays.

*(*ED *is totally thrown. He notices for the first time what* DON
is wearing.)

ED: You're wearing a blazer.

DON: My courtroom blazer. I figured you'd come in
here with guns-a-blazing, trying to change my mind.
So I got ready.

ED: Don.

DON: It's not about the pain. You understand that don't you? The pain is bad. But this is about my daughter and that child.

ED: I know, I know you're afraid you'll hurt them but—

DON: "But won't *this* hurt them Don, what you're planning to do?" That's your next question. And I answer, no, not physically. "What about emotionally?" And I answer, she'll be spared. Spared the pain of having to visit her father in some nursing facility, him not even knowing who she is. Seeing me deteriorate, stink from sitting in my own feces, slack-jawed and drooling from all the meds they pump into me to make sure I don't injure the staff. Because those places, they're not prepared to handle guys like me with dementia. Younger guys, strong men and their mood shifts. What are they going to do, what can they do, other than sedate me? No, I'll spare her all of that.

ED: Wow. You seem really good today.

DON: Some days are like that. Might last the day, or an hour, or ten minutes. I never know.

ED: I've heard grandparents talk about grandchildren as giving them a whole new life. A new purpose.

DON: Ed. Listen to me. Listen to me carefully now: I will not. Put that child. In jeopardy.

ED: I hear you, I do. But the Don Devers I grew up watching, if there was one thing I knew, that I could count on, that I modeled myself after, it was that Don Devers never gives up. He never gives up.

DON: And what's wrong with giving up? In many cultures giving up is considered positive. Enlightened even.

(Full lawyer mode)

But we're not one of those cultures. Because here ladies
and gentlemen of the jury, here we are taught we
must never give up; we must always have a goal, an
endzone, something to strive for, and we must not give
up until we get there. No matter what the obstacles.
No matter how many times you're hit, knocked back,
tackled, cut into, you keep driving forward. Over and
over, banging against that wall until it gives, even
if it doesn't. And we've been convinced this is the
righteous path, the American Way, when in fact it's the
very definition of insanity. Doing the same thing over
and over again, expecting a different result. Don't stop.
Keep banging away. Banging away. Banging away.
Well that much banging takes a toll. And I'm pretty
sure you, sir, can relate to that. With your years of
banging your own head, trying to break through that
sportswriting wall. It takes a toll, doesn't it?

(ED *says nothing, struck to the core.* DON *is pleased with his
courtroom victory.*)

DON: *Woo-ee*! I tell you, after pulling my pants down, I
feel better. I feel better and freer than I have in a long
time. It's like when you finally leave the game and you
don't have to go to mini-camp or work your tail off
in the off-season anymore. You can go out with your
daughter and eat that ice cream. Man, some guys, they
just balloon up. They just love it, letting go, giving all
that up, getting fat. Fat and happy. Let's get fat and
happy, Ed. Whatya say?

ED: *(Dazed)* I say...I say, what you did there, that...that
was like an *anti*-lockerroom speech.
(Tiny beat)
And I think I'm having a panic attack.

(DON *grabs a pill bottle and tosses it to* ED. ED *looks up at
him.*)

DON: Xanax. Take one.

Maybe two.

Scene 3

(SARAH *and* STEPHANIE *in their familiar positions. They munch on the occasional chip as they work. A beat or two like this, then* SARAH *finishes something, turns the tablet to* STEPHANIE.)

SARAH: What do you think?

STEPHANIE: *(Not looking)* I love it.

SARAH: You're not even looking.

STEPHANIE: *(She looks)* Awesome. Encouragement, encouragement, support, support.

SARAH: Wow.

STEPHANIE: Sorry, that was bitchy. I'm uncomfortable and where's Ed and eating these fucking things doesn't help.

SARAH: It's Kale. It's a superfood.

STEPHANIE: It's nasty. And desiccating it doesn't help. Where the fuck is he?

(SARAH *and* STEPHANIE *both hear something.*)

STEPHANIE: About time.

(ED *moseys in high as a kite, holding a brown shopping bag.*)

STEPHANIE: How's my dad?

SARAH: How'd the speech go?

ED: Awesome and awesome. He called my speech high level. Then he made one of his own, which basically altered my consciousness. Your dad, he's like… a lawyer-philosopher. And look. I brought you cake.

(ED *pulls a box from the bag, drops it down in front of* SARAH *and* STEPHANIE.)

STEPHANIE: Shut up.

SARAH: You brought us cake?

ED: I brought you cake.

STEPHANIE: Well if she doesn't blow you for this, I will.

SARAH: Nice.

STEPHANIE: *(Her explanation)* Cake.

SARAH: *(Agrees with the explanation)* Cake.
(To ED*)*
I can't believe how well this is going.

*(*ED *hands both* SARAH *and* STEPHANIE *a spoon. This will not be a slice by slice affair.)*

ED: Arm yourselves.

SARAH: Sit with us?

ED: In the vaunted Sarah Stephanie good time bonding bubble? Don't mind if I do.

*(*ED *drops down, sitting with* SARAH *and* STEPHANIE *for the first time. He takes a moment to enjoy it.)*

(He reaches over to the cakebox and slowly, ceremoniously unties the string, tantalizing them. He opens the lid. SARAH *and* STEPHANIE *stare down at the holy grail, mesmorized.)*

STEPHANIE: Let's do this.

*(*SARAH *and* STEPHANIE *dive in.)*

SARAH: Mmmmm.

STEPHANIE: Ohhhhhh.

SARAH: Caaaaake.

STEPHANIE: Caaaaake.

*(*SARAH *and* STEPHANIE *take another spoonful, silently savoring it in their mouths. Ecstacy)*

STEPHANIE: Well, smell us. One big, happy cake-eating family.

(To SARAH*)*

A person could get used to this. Imagine it? The four of us. You and Ed, me and Jimmyjane.

I mean, check out your man. Sitting here, all happy-go-lucky.

ED: The Xanax really helps.

SARAH: The Xanax?

ED: Don gave me one. Ok, two.
(He cracks up, DON *style. Decides to take a bite of cake.)*

SARAH: Why did Don give you two Xanax?

ED: *(Mouth full of cake)* Anxiety. Panic. 'Cause Don, he took everything I've ever thought and just flipped it upside down. Whoop. But I'm good now. Really good.
(Suddenly jumps up)
Ok-dokey, gotta go, perishables in the trunk.

STEPHANIE: What do you mean perishables?

ED: Well, some perishables, some not. A very long list your dad gave me.

STEPHANIE: You're telling me my father asked you to purchase food for him that's not vacuum-sealed in a can?

ED: I'm feeding everyone! Ed Ryan feeds everyone!

SARAH: Ed, are you alright?

ED: I think so.

SARAH: What do you mean he flipped your world upside down?

ED: I mean, every time I see him, he says something to make me see the world in a whole new way. Banging is insanity. Giving up, enlightenment. It's…wow. Mind-altering. And a bit unsetting.
(Laughs)
More than a bit.

Well alrighty then, enjoy the cake. Oh, and don't wait up. Don and I, we're having a sleepover!

(ED *exits.* SARAH *and* STEPHANIE *turn to each other.*)

STEPHANIE: *It's going well.* Thank God, thank God, thank God

SARAH: I guess, though that seemed…

STEPHANIE: No. Don't. Don't overthink it. It's going well.

SARAH: You sure?

STEPHANIE: *It's amazing.*
Though with him out tonight, you need a date.

SARAH: A date?

STEPHANIE: I've got Jimmyjane. And you, you'll have Jimmyjane's brother.

SARAH: Oh my God.

STEPHANIE: I'm just saying, you might want to get acquainted. Who knows how many nights those two are going to spend together now.

SARAH: Well just until Sunday.

STEPHANIE: Stay longer.
Wait, wait, wait, don't say anything, don't say anything until you hear me out. Ok, here it is: you and I, we continue our work, and I continue to pay you, so you can start to dig yourself out of debt. And while we're doing that, Ed can keep on visiting my father.

SARAH: You're not serious? I don't think—

STEPHANIE: Okay hold on, wait, there's something else.

Okay, it's like this. If I was a different person, *which I'm not*, I would say something sappy right now. Like…it would mean a lot to me if you were here. You know… "by my side". When this sucker busts out.

SARAH: What do you mean? Like literally "by your side"?

STEPHANIE: Yes. Like literally by my side. During birth. As long you don't talk about Roses unfurling.
And when the jailbreak happens, I'll need someone I trust, to hold the little criminal. Rock him to sleep. So I can nap. Or cry. Or something.

SARAH: You'd trust me to do that?

STEPHANIE: Yes. I would. I do.

(SARAH *takes this in.*)

STEPHANIE: See? You have to stay. Come on. Whatya say? Stay for a while.

Scene 4

(DON's *condo. An excessive amount of candy spread across the floor, the side table, everywhere. A six pack of Coke, an empty pint of ice cream, a whip cream bottle or two.* DON *sits in his chair,* ED *on the floor, the candy master. They gleefully binge-eat like two kids on Halloween.)*

ED: What's next?

DON: A Mounds. Pass me a Mounds.

ED: Not Almond Joy?

DON: Almond Joy's got nuts.

ED: Mounds don't.

DON: Because…

DON & ED: *(Singing)*
Sometimes you feel like a nut, sometimes you don't.

(DON *and* ED *crack up. Sugar high. And Xanax. They eat their candy as they talk.)*

DON: Interesting how relevant that song has become for me.

ED: Are you still feeling…

DON: Good. Clear.

ED: Mounds-y?

DON: Not like a nut.

ED: Any idea why?

DON: None.

ED: Because if you did, if you could isolate the factors…

DON: Good try. But I've tried everything, believe me. Kept charts. Different foods, meds, med combinations, exercise, P T, O T, C B T, fresh air, classical music. No pattern. It just comes and goes. Like someone else is at the control panel. So what haven't we tried?

(ED *searches through the assortment.*)

ED: Pop Rocks?

DON: Bring it on.

ED: You sure? Mikey died from Pop Rocks.

DON: We'll wash 'em down with a Coke.

ED: You madman.

(ED *pops open a Coke. He pours some in a plastic cup for* DON *and some into a cup for himself.*)

ED: What's with all the paper and plastic?

DON: My last nurse. I launched a glass at him. Fifteen stitches on his chin. Though he still came back for one more day, brave soul. Replaced all the glass and ceramics with plastic and paper.

(DON *and* ED *raise their cups and open their packets.*)

DON: To Mikey.

ED: To Mikey.

(DON *and* ED *pour Pop Rocks in their mouths then chase it with Coke. They experience it fully, all the crazy intense popping in their mouths, the facial expressions and vocalization that follow. Have fun playing with this and the sound it makes. Take your time.)*

DON: Wow.

ED: He likes it, Mikey likes it!

DON: *(A grin spreads across his face)* Let's do it again.

(DON *and* ED *do it again. Pop rocks, Coke chaser. Intense. Popping, popping, popping sounds. They crack up. After a few beats of this fun…)*

ED: Don?

DON: No, no more. Well both explode.

ED: No, would tell me. Tell me exactly how you plan to, you know, do the thing that you're going to do?

DON: Are you trying to ruin our fat and happy giving up party?

ED: Please.

(A beat)

DON: A bunch of guys shot themselves, but I don't like guns so that's out. Bunch of them did it that way, though. Dave Duerson, da Bears.

ED: Andre Waters, Eagles.

DON: Ray Easterling, Falcons.

ED: Junior Seau, Chargers.

DON: Duerson and Seau specifically shot themselves in the chest so their brains could be studied.

ED: So…?

DON: Look at the cart. Plenty here. I'll just wash them all down with something toxic. A nice anti-freeze maybe. Worked for Terry Long. Steelers.

ED: *He drank antifreeze?*

DON: Yep.

ED: My god, Don, that, that's, that's…

DON: Is that the stutter?

ED: It's shock. Believe me, you'd know if I was stuttering.

DON: That bad, huh?

ED: It doesn't matter. I mean, compared to what you're—

DON: I'm asking. Really.

ED: Okay. Well it wasn't just tripping on a sound or a word. It was more like a full-on mouth seizure. Like I was chewing on the sound. Off to one side of my mouth. Like…
(He demonstrates. It's grotesque.)

DON: Yikes.

ED: I'm not exaggerating either.
(Chuckles)
It was awful.

DON: Kids went after you for it?

ED: These two kids, twins, the Tobin twins. When I went into my stutter, they'd punch me, or kick me, or shove me into a locker. Said they were trying to help. That I was like a jukebox with a record skipping. They were giving me a kick to get my record back on track. A-holes. I didn't want open my mouth, at all. I hated talking. Even aside from the stutter, I never felt like I'd…say the right thing in the moment. I'd go home and torture myself, revise it in my head over and over.

I still hate it. Talking. I mean, when someone talks
to you, you have to respond. Right then. You can't
sit there for twenty minutes, composing. You have
to talk. And what comes out of your mouth, it's like,
like a first draft. And the first draft of anything is shit.
Hemmingway said that. So it's like, when I talk, when
anybody talks, it's like we're all spewing our noxious,
first draft shit all over the place.

DON: That why you started to write?

ED: I thought I could give up talking.

(DON *raises his cup.*)

DON: To giving up.
(*He drinks. Small beat*)
Tell me.

ED: Tell you…?

DON: How is she?

ED: Stephanie? She's happy. That you and I are
spending time. That you're not isolated and alone. That
your eating something other than Pringles. Course I
haven't told her your intentions.

DON: And her pregnancy? My…grandson.

ED: Could be any day now. Actually, her official due
date is the same day as the Superbo—you knew that.
Of course you knew that.

(DON *smiles.*)

ED: You really want me to take video? You can't
actually want that. I don't believe it.

DON: Believe it.

ED: And then post it where? youtube? Twitter?

DON: Whatever makes it public. So maybe some of the
younger guys will walk away, save themselves.

ED: He's going to see it, you know? Some day. Your grandson.

DON: That's the idea.

ED: That's awful.

DON: The boy has a football player for a grandfather and a football player for a deadbeat father. He's got it on both sides. Maybe this way, he'll never even think about strapping on a helmet.

ED: That's...are you kidding? You can just have Stephanie forbid it. Have her forbid him from ever playing.

DON: Yeah? Well my mother forbade me from playing. Did you know that? Wouldn't even let me play pickup games down at the park when I was in junior high. But I'd play anyway, without her knowing. And sometimes my clothes would get torn. So I'd bring a bag with me, to the park, with a change of clothes and a sewing kit. And after the game, I'd sit right down on a bench or a rock and sew up the tears in my pants or shirt. The other kids got on me about it, in school mostly, since I was the only male to enroll in home ec class. But I learned to sew. And do my own laundry. And I came home and told my mother she worked too hard, and anytime she needed any sewing done, or the laundry, I was the man to do it. Which I did. All to hide the fact that I was playing pickup football in the park.

(Small beat)

ED: What if I say no? What if I just don't show on that day?

DON: It's going to happen whether you do or not. The question is whether my number one fan will grant Don Devers his dying wish.
(He punctuates this by spraying a stream of whipped cream in his mouth. He smiles.)

ED: My God, you must have been a hell of a lawyer.

DON: I was. Until I started forgetting court dates and client names. Or when I couldn't remember which was my car in the parking lot. I didn't remember what it looked like, so I thought it was stolen. Accused my colleagues of stealing it.

ED: Do you miss it?

DON: My car?

ED: Being a lawyer.

DON: Sometimes.

ED: Football.

DON: Desperately.

ED: What do you miss most?

DON: The contact. The daily, physical contact. Knowing I was alive because I had a body and that body came in contact, in fierce, primal contact, with other bodies.
(Small beat, then he pushes himself up.)
Come on.

ED: What?

DON: Hit me.

ED: No way.

DON: Then let me tackle you.

ED: Can you do that? Isn't it going to…

DON: Hurt like hell? Probably. Do further damage to my back? Or neck? Or knees? Quite possibly. Come on.

ED: You can't run.

DON: Here.
(He gets his walker, shuffles away from the chair a bit. He moves to the side of his walker, holding on to it with one hand, the rest of his body clear of it.)

Try to run past me. We're at the goal-line.

ED: While I see how you might mistake me for an
N F L running back...

DON: Come on, bring it to me! Oh, and make sure you
move the candy out of the way, I wouldn't want you to
trip.

(ED *looks at* DON *a beat, highly dubious. He clears a runway
through the candy on the floor.*)

ED: Okay.

(ED *starts a kind of slow-motion jog to* DON.)

DON: No, no, no. *For real.* Run by me. Try to score. This
is your chance to say you scored against Don Devers.

ED: Okay. Okay...here I...

(ED *tries to run by.* DON *uses just his forearm and knocks it
against* ED's *shoulder.* ED *goes flying down to the ground.
He lies there prostrate a beat, stunned. Suddenly he starts
laughing.*)

ED: Holy shit. Football's dangerous.

DON: You okay?

ED: Say it? Would you say it me?

DON: I'm glad you're all right. But son I should let you
know, next time you try to run it past me...

Don & ED: You'll get more of the same!

DON: You betcha.

ED: That was amazing! Thank you.
Are you okay? Did it hurt?

DON: Not too bad.

ED: Well I'll never try to score against you again. I give
up.

(DON *raises his cup.*)

DON: To giving up!

(ED *tries to sit up, but falls back flat.*)

DON: You okay?

ED: I think I'm having a Xanax-sugar-combo-crash. You mind if I just stay down here a bit?

DON: Be my guest.

Scene 5

(*In dim light we hear a buzzing sound. Lights come up enough to see* SARAH, *a vibrator happily buzzing in her hand. She contemplates it, this foreign entity. Turns it on and off, plays with the settings. She's startled by one of the more intense ones. She tries another one. That, too, freaks her out. Maybe she tries another [a vibrator lazzi]. Eventually, she fumbles her way to a more benign setting. Okay. She takes a deep breath, and moves the vibrator down below.*)

Scene 6

(*Lights up. The next day. Early morning.* ED *is passed out on the floor.* DON *sits upright in his chair, eyes open, staring straight ahead, dazed, sleepless, the taser on his lap.*)

(*Trance-like, he reaches for the whip cream bottle, sprays some in his mouth. The sound rouses* ED. *He slowly wakes. Hungover. He orients himself. Sees the wrappers and empty cartons everywhere.*)

ED: Well. That was a party.
You're still at it I see. You keep going. I'll do clean-up duty.
(*He cleans up.*)
 Can you imagine how much fun this would be to do with your grandchild. I'm just saying. Halloween

together. The two of you. Spilling all your candy out
on the floor, making trades. Comparing notes on which
house gave you full sized versus bite sized. Bingeing,
the permissive grandfather letting him eat everything
at once.

(ED *reaches out for a wrapper by* DON'*s side table. As he
does,* DON *grabs his wrist. Hard)*

ED: Woh. Don, I'm sorry. I'm sorry if that was…

(DON *holds onto* ED.)

ED: Don?

(DON *grips* ED'*s wrist tighter.)*

ED: Ow. Don.

DON: I told you didn't I? You come back this way and
you get more of the same.

ED: *(In pain)* Don, let go.

DON: Fifteen stitches not enough for you?

ED: Don, it's me. It's Ed. I'm not your nurse.

(DON *twists* ED'*s wrist.)*

DON: I don't need a nurse!

ED: Don! Don! Check your Post-it. Look at the Post-it.
It's me, it's Ed.

(DON *doesn't budge. He tightens his grip.* ED *in pain,
desperately searches for what to do. He reaches for the taser.*
DON *grabs it first.)*

DON: You think this will stop me? Not me.

(DON *tases* ED *who screams out and drops to the floor.*
DON *still holds his twisted wrist as he tases him again.* ED
screams. He tases him again. Then again. ED *screaming in
pain. Finally,* DON *lets go.)*

DON: A-11. I park it there every day. You stole it, I
know you did.

(ED *dazed, gets to his feet, and manages to stumble out the door and escape.*)

DON: I park it there every day. I WANT MY CAR BACK!

Scene 7

(*Later that day.* SARAH *and* STEPHANIE. STEPHANIE *in pain.* SARAH *helping her shift her position.*)

SARAH: Some women have back labor. It's pretty common. I'm just saying…

STEPHANIE: It's not a contraction if it stops when I move. It's not. *It's not, okay?* But nice to see you so excited by my pain.

(ED *enters, his arm in a cast. He's all purpose.*)

SARAH: Oh my God.

STEPHANIE: Oh shit.

SARAH: My god, Ed, what happened?

ED: He broke my arm, tased me, several times.

SARAH: This is Don, Don did this?

ED: He gave his nurse fifteen stitches, he shoved his wife against the wall, gave her a concussion which caused her car crash.

STEPHANIE: *What?* He thinks that's why she crashed?

ED: He feels responsible. And he's probably right.

STEPHANIE: *He's not.*

SARAH: (*To* STEPHANIE) You never told me he was violent.

STEPHANIE: Because he isn't.

SARAH: *Look at Ed.* (*To* ED) Are you okay? Can I get you anything? Do you want to—

ED: He launched a walker at my head the first day, held me at taser point the second.

(*To* STEPHANIE)

Your father is dangerous and he is violent and he knows it.

SARAH: Why didn't you tell me? This whole time? *Why didn't either of you tell me?*

ED: Because this isn't about me, it's about Don.

STEPHANIE: That's exactly right. Now listen, I am about to go out of commission here very soon, so I need you to tell me if I, *or you,* need to do something before that happens.

SARAH: Ed's not going back there.

STEPHANIE: Yes he is.

SARAH: No he's fucking not.

ED: Yes I fucking am. Probably not tomorrow. Or the next day. But Sunday. I'll be there Sunday. I have to, I really think I do, or I should, or I don't fucking know but I think I'm going to. I really do.

SARAH: No, there's no way you're going back there.

ED: (*Turning back to* STEPHANIE) *Listen to me.* Your father is going downhill and he knows it. He feels it, that he's turning into something else, something completely opposite from the man he used to be and he's asked me to make that public, to make it very public, so he can help others, so he can do something good, something important, before he...

STEPHANIE: Before he what?

ED: (*This is it*) At halftime of the Superbowl your father is going to kill himself and he asked me to record it then post it online.

STEPHANIE: Is that your idea of a joke?

ED: He wants it seen, so maybe some players will walk away, or never even strap on a helmet, *so his grandson* will never strap on a helmet.

STEPHANIE: Assuming you're not fucking with me right now—

ED: I'm not.

STEPHANIE: —did he say this to you this morning, because he was obviously not in his right mind.

ED: He asked me two days ago when he was clear as a bell.

STEPHANIE: *Two days ago?!*

ED: I thought I could convince him not to! But he's going to do it no matter what.

STEPHANIE: *(Getting up) Are you out of your fucking mind?!*

SARAH: Please tell me you're not serious about this?

STEPHANIE: Call 911, call 911 *right now.*

ED: And have them tranquilize him like some wild beast. Sedate him for the rest of his life?

STEPHANIE: Better than him being dead!

ED: Is it?!

STEPHANIE: He's getting better. You're helping him get better.

ED: He's not getting better and he's not going to! Have you read anything about any of the former players? It's downhill from here. And it is ugly.

STEPHANIE: You think I don't know that? What the hell do you think I've been doing with my life? The little I have of it. I've been taking care of him. Setting up his nursing care, moving him into that apartment, hiring contractors to raise the height of the kitchen counters because he couldn't fucking bend at the waist. So don't tell me what it's like for my father because you don't know shit about it.

ED: I know that man deserves to be honored, to have his final wishes honored.

STEPHANIE: *My father does not give up!*

ED: *Well he sure as hell wants to!* He's scared to death that he'll do something to harm his grandchild. Or you. I didn't believe he'd be capable of that, I truly didn't. Until now. *(To* SARAH*)* The real reason he won't see her.

STEPHANIE: It wasn't his fault. He was upset about the pregnancy.

SARAH: Oh my God, he did something to you.

STEPHANIE: It was nothing. It's not like I doubled over or anything.

SARAH: He punched you in the stomach, did he punch you in the stomach?

STEPHANIE: *I was fine, the baby was fine.* I told him I was fine!

(She gets up, starts off.)

SARAH: *Where are you going?*

STEPHANIE: I have to see him.

SARAH: Are you crazy, he could hurt you. Hurt the baby.

STEPHANIE: Take me there. Take me there right the fuck now, while there's still…oh no, oh please no, oh fuck. Fuck, fuck, fuck, fuck, *fuck.*
(She sits right down. Covers her legs and crosses them.)
My pants are wet. My pants are very fucking wet.

SARAH: Did you pee yourself?

STEPHANIE: No, I didn't pee myself *I've done a thousand fucking kegels!*

SARAH: Your water. That means you're on the clock.

STEPHANIE: No shit!

SARAH: Ok, just calm down. We'll get you comfortable and I'll call your doctor.
(To ED*)*
You can't go back there.

ED: He's going to do it whether I'm there or not.

STEPHANIE: *Then stall him.* Stall him until I can get there—oh fuck.

(Contraction. Intense pain. STEPHANIE *can't talk, totally inside herself.* ED *and* SARAH *watch her.)*

(Pause)

(Then it passes. STEPHANIE *silent, jolted by the intensity of the pain. She stares down at the floor, trying not to panic.)*

SARAH: You are not doing this. Tell her that. *Ed.*

ED: Look, nothing's going to happen until Sunday. Okay? There's still time.

*(*STEPHANIE *manages a tiny nod.* ED *and* SARAH *go to help her up.* SARAH *leads her off to the bedroom.)*

SARAH: Your cervix is like a rosebud…

*(*SARAH *and* STEPHANIE *exit.)*

*(*ED *alone. He sits down. A small beat. He slams his fist down.)*

Scene 8

(Morning. Thirty-six hours later. STEPHANIE*'s condo.* ED *sits alone, staring into space, a brown shopping bag in front of him.)*

(After a beat, SARAH *enters. She stands there a moment, looks at* ED.*)*

SARAH: I think that's where I left you.

ED: Probably.
How is she?

SARAH: I'm the only one at the hospital with her. Thirty-six hours and...no one. She wasn't lying about that. She is alone. She is definitely alone.

ED: And the baby?

SARAH: The baby's...incredible. Incredible.

*(*ED *smiles.)*

SARAH: I thought I'd take a nap then go back again. Get her dressed, hold the baby, try to be a help.

ED: Nice of you.

(A beat)

SARAH: I'm still in awe. She had all this tearing and... I don't know if I have that kind of strength.

ED: You do. I know you do.

(A beat)

SARAH: What's in the bag, or shouldn't I ask?

ED: Duct tape.
Anti-freeze.
(Tiny beat, awed)
Talk about fatherhood. Don Devers, a man who'll do anything to protect his family, even if it's from himself.

SARAH: Ed?

ED: What?

SARAH: I don't want you to protect us from you.

ED: Aren't you dizzy from it? You fall in love with this guy for how he tries and tries to be the man he wants to be, but with all the support and encouragement you have to constantly put forth, doesn't it feel like you're just ramming your head into me over and over. That takes a toll, doesn't it? That much ramming? Maybe the only sane thing for you to do is…

SARAH: What? Give up? Stop? No. No, that doesn't feel like the sanest option right now.

(A beat)

Let's stay.

ED: Stay…?

SARAH: Here. With Stephanie.

ED: Are you kidding?

SARAH: We need help. And so does she.

ED: Sarah.

SARAH: I know it sounds crazy, I know. But think about it. We could ditch the apartment. Live here for free. I keep working for Stephanie and then, when the baby comes, we might actually have something. A place to stay and a little something on top of that.

ED: And me? What do I do in this scenario?

SARAH: You could look for a job or maybe you'd want to, I don't know…stay home? With the baby. Babies. I don't know, *I don't know*, but maybe that would…give you something. I mean, putting someone else before yourself, the way you have with Don. That kind of devotion. You have that.

(A beat)

Ed, what the hell else are we going to do?

ED: I don't know.

(Small beat)

I suppose it's not the worst idea in the world. Though she's sure not going to want us around after this, after her father… Seems like that might be a dealbreaker.

SARAH: Exactly.

Ed, you're not really going to do this. I don't believe it.

ED: It's not up to me.

(A beat. Two. SARAH lingers a moment, then exits.)

(ED closes his eyes a beat, then stands up, grabs the bag, and heads out.)

Scene 9

(DON's apartment. Later. He in his chair, upright. This is Game Day. Nothing indecisive, nothing hesitant, nothing sentimental or scared. This is him as he was when he was on the field or in the courtroom. Focussed and confident, able to toss out a joke or two. He's ready to go.)

(He's popped off the tops of most of his pill bottles. A Gatorade bottle filled with a murky liquid sits next to him. ED, at a bit of distance, takes video with his phone.)

(DON takes the cap off another bottle. He spills the pills onto a paper plate and uses a spoon to crush them up. He folds the plate and funnels the crushed-up pills into the Gatorade bottle.)

DON: That should be enough.

ED: I'd say so.

DON: Then I'll chase it down with this fine bouquet of anti-freeze.

(He swirls the antifreeze-Gatorade as if in a wine glass. He chuckles.)

ED: Do you want to watch any of the game? I can stream it on my phone.

DON: No need.

ED: So…the duct tape now?

DON: Yes siree Bob.

(ED *puts his phone down and picks up the roll of duct tape.*)

ED: *(Indicating his armcast)* I may need you to start the roll for me.

DON: How'd you do it?

ED: Do…?

DON: Your arm, how'd you break it?

ED: *(Stunned, a beat)* It…it was…it was an accident. No one's fault.
Hey, you know what? Would you sign it for me? The cast?

DON: Of course.

(DON *takes a pen from his table. Signs* ED's *cast.*)

ED: Thank you.

DON: You're quite welcome.

(A beat)

ED: Ready?

DON: Yes sir.

(ED *hands* DON *the roll to start it.*)

DON: It was a good idea on my part. The duct tape. If I do say so myself. It'll keep me in the chair. Keep me in the frame.

(DON *starts the roll then hands it back to* ED.)

DON: There you go.

(ED *hesitates.*)

ED: Did I tell you that you got me kicked out of Sunday School?

DON: I did?

ED: They asked us to write an essay about God. I wrote about you.

DON: Swelling my head won't fix my condition you know.

ED: I told them you did everything for me that God could do.

You gave me an origin story.

You gave me a moral compass.

And you gave me a power greater than myself to look up to, to revere.

(This sits between DON and ED beat. Then DON looks to ED who accedes and begins the duct-taping. We hear only the horrible sound of ripping adhesion as he circles around and around and around the chair. Loops and loops of duct tape secure DON's upper arms and torso to the chair. Only his arms below the elbow are left free to pivot. Next ED circles DON's legs, securing them to the chair.)

(When all is done, the image is of a man nearly completely mummified by duct tape. Bound to the chair, looking as if he's part of it.)

ED: How's that?

(DON tries to move his torso, his legs. He can't. Not a single inch.)

DON: I believe King Kong couldn't free himself from such handy-work.

(ED comes around to DON's front. DON places his wrists together. ED tapes them, careful to allow DON's hands to still pivot at the joint. When he's done DON tries to move his wrists apart. He can't.)

DON: I'll never tell you where the jewels are. Never.
(He cracks up. Stops)
A dry run.
(With his wrists taped, he cups his hands as if around a bottle. With his elbows left free to bend, he brings the pretend bottle to his mouth, as if taking a drink.)

Good enough.

Alright, Mr DeMille, I'm ready for my close-up.

(He takes one big breath, then nods to ED.*)*

(Soberly)

Okay.

*(*ED *nods. He moves over to* DON*'s cart. He wheels it behind the chair and out of* DON*'s reach.)*

DON: Mr Ryan, what are you doing?

ED: I just need a minute to set up. I wouldn't want you to start drinking before I'm ready.

(He makes a call on his cell.)

DON: Good. I thought maybe you were pulling a fast one on me.

ED: *(Into his phone)* Ready.

(On that, STEPHANIE *enters the apartment. She stands at the threshold, holding her baby boy swaddled in a blanket.* DON *immediately turns his head away.)*

DON: No. *No, no, no!* Get out. Get her out of here!

ED: Don. You're secured. You can't do anything. You can't possibly do anything.

STEPHANIE: Dad, I have your grandson here. Would you like to meet him?

*(*DON *keeps his head turned away. Says nothing)*

STEPHANIE: Or put another way, if you are going to kill yourself, you're going to hold your damn grandson before you do, even if I have to strap him to you with duct tape.

*(*STEPHANIE *slowly crosses the length of the room.* DON *keeps his head turned, averting his eyes.* ED *moves back, quietly taking video.)*

*(*STEPHANIE *moves right in front of the chair and stands before* DON. DON *refuses to look as she kneels down and*

gently places the baby in the crook of his heavily duct-taped arms. We hold this image a beat. Duct-taped DON, *baby in his arms.)*

*(*STEPHANIE *supports the baby's head, gently holding him in place.)*

STEPHANIE: You know who that is baby boy? That's your grandpa. Your Grandpa Don.

(With all his might, DON *battles the urge to look at the baby. Eventually he loses. He slowly looks down at the child in his arms.)*

*(*DON *breaks. The first time we've seen this Titan succumb to emotion. His face crumples and he begins to sob.)*

(After a moment, he starts to get a hold of himself, taking deep shaky breathes.)

DON: I am so, so very sorry.

STEPHANIE: You have nothing to be sorry about. You hear me? Nothing. You are a good, good man.

*(*DON *gazes down at his grandchild.)*

DON: He's beautiful.

STEPHANIE: He better be. Fucker tore me up coming out.

*(*DON *smiles. The daughter he knows and loves.)*

DON: What's his name? And if you were silly enough to name him after his dumb old grandpa you're going to have to change it.

STEPHANIE: Of course I didn't name him after you, you arrogant bastard.

DON: Good.

STEPHANIE: As if you could make me change it anyway.

DON: Well?

STEPHANIE: Daniel. His name is Daniel.

DON: Well Daniel, I'm…I'm very pleased to make your acquaintance.

STEPHANIE: You hear that, little one? Those are called manners. One of the many things I hope you get from your grandpa instead of me.

DON: Hey now, you listen to me young man. You've got a darn good mother right there. She's a special one. Don't ever let her forget it.

(DON *and* STEPHANIE *look at one another a silent beat.*)

(*Then* DON *nods to her. It's time.*)

(STEPHANIE *stares at him, then leans over and picks up baby Daniel. She holds his little face up to* DON's.)

(DON *pushes his chin forward and kisses the boy on the forehead. Then he turns his head and looks away.*)

STEPHANIE: Every time.
We could do it just like this.
A roll of duct tape.
4.99 at Target.
20 for a six-pack.

(STEPHANIE *leans in and kisses* DON. *She turns and quickly leaves before she completely loses it, not knowing if this is the last time she'll see her father.*)

(*As soon as she's gone, the flood gates open.* DON *howls to the heavens and beyond. An absolute tornado of emotion. Everything, all of it pouring out of him.*)

(ED *silently records all of it. It goes on for a while.*)

(*Finally, finally* DON *wears down. Gasping for air, his eyes wild*)

(*Silence*)

ED: I'm sorry, I just, I had to give you every chance to change your mind.

(DON *stares at* ED.)

ED: He's a beautiful grandson, Don.

(DON *doesn't answer.*)

ED: Amazing isn't it?

(DON *doesn't answer.*)

ED: Daniel Devers.

DON: Very clever. That's very clever. Pulling out all the stops now. But that's crossing the line, don't you think? Making something like that up. A grandson.

ED: Don?

(*Heartbroken, realizing*)

Oh, no.

No.

Oh God, please, please, please no.

(DON *just stares at* ED, *confused.*)

ED: Don…

(ED *goes over to him. He finds a section of the video on his phone. He turns the phone to* DON *and plays it for him.* DON *watches the video, expressionless at first. Then disbelief. Then a giant grin spreads across his face. He starts laughing. He looks up at* ED, *overjoyed.*)

ED: You met your grandson.

DON: I met my grandson.

(*Suddenly the joy turns to panic.*)

DON: Did I…? Did anything…?

ED: No. Nothing bad happened. Not a thing.

(*Joy.* DON *laughs, he cries, he's utterly overwhelmed by emotion. A moment or two then he takes big gulps of air, trying to calm himself. Eventually he does. Continuing with deep breaths*)

ED: Want to see it again?

(DON *says nothing.*)

ED: I can play it again.

DON: Play what?

ED: The video.

DON: What video?

(DON just looks at him, blank. No recollection. He's gone. Short circuited by the overwhelming, volcanic emotion of all that's happened.)

(ED looks at him, heartbroken.)

ED: I guess you were right. It gets worse. Precipitously. But you know what? You were right about something else.
You're greatest moment *is* yet to come.
(He holds up the phone.)
And it will come again.
And again.
And again.
And again.

(ED resets the video, pushes play, and hands it to DON.)

(DON watches the video, once again experiencing all the joy of it as if for the first time. Because for him it is.)

(With DON staring down at the video, laughing, full of joy, ED quietly begins to remove the duct tape from around him. The sounds of DON's laughter. The sounds of duct tape.)

(Laughter)

(Duct tape)

(Laughter)

(Duct tape)

(Lights fade)

END OF PLAY

PRODUCTION NOTES

I strongly recommend using a profusion of duct tape, really mummify Don to the chair. If not, if only a few loops are made with the tape, then the idea that the tape will really secure this force of a man will seem silly. That, and if there's not enough tape, it runs the risk of the audience being distracted, wondering if the tape will come off or the actor will break free accidentally. In past productions, we found non-residue duct tape and made sure Don was duct-taped over long sleeves. A scissor was hidden in the back of the recliner so once in blackout, the actor playing Ed could cut away the duct tape he hasn't already unraveled.

In each of the initial productions, we decided to have Don onstage the whole time so as not to ruin the illusion of his physical decimation by having him enter and exit. If he did exit during intermission, he moved off (slowly) in character.

www.ingramcontent.com/pod-product-compliance
Lightning Source LLC
Chambersburg PA
CBHW052207090426
42741CB00010B/2438